How To Attract Anything You Want In Life

DISCLAIMER AND TERMS OF USE AGREEMENT:

(Please Read This Before Using This Report)

This information in this course is for educational and informational purposes only. The content is not presented by a professional, and therefore the information in this course should not be considered a substitute for professional advice. Always seek the advice of someone qualified in this field for any questions you may have.

The author and publisher of this course and the accompanying materials have used their best efforts in preparing this course. The author and publisher make no representation or warranties with respect to the accuracy, applicability, fitness, or completeness of the contents of this course. The information contained in this course is strictly for educational purposes. Therefore, if you wish to apply ideas contained in this course, you are taking full responsibility for your actions.

The author and publisher disclaim any warranties (express or implied), merchantability, or fitness for any particular purpose. The author and publisher shall in no event be held liable to any party for any direct, indirect, punitive, special, incidental or other consequential damages arising directly or indirectly from any use of this material, which is provided "as is", and without warranties.

As always, the advice of a competent legal, tax, accounting, medical or other professional should be sought. The author and publisher do not warrant the performance, effectiveness or applicability of any sites listed or linked to in this course.

All links are for information purposes only and are not warranted for content, accuracy or any other implied or explicit purpose.

This report is © Copyrighted. No part of this may be copied, or changed in any format, or used in any way other than what is outlined within this course under any circumstances. Violators would be prosecuted severely.

Contents

The Law of Attraction Can Build Your Business

The Law of Attraction And Home Based Business

The Law of Attraction And Getting Clients

The Law of Attraction And Network Marketing

The Law of Attraction In Sales And Marketing

Laws of Attraction - The Alpha Male Mentality

Law of Attraction - Study of how different cultures react on dating

The Law of Attraction and Your Body

Law of Attraction - Raising your Attraction Potential

Some Fascinating Books on the Law of Attraction

The Law of Attraction

Law of Attraction - How the Human Race chooses their mates

How to Compete with the Alpha Male

Scientific study of male and female interactions

The Consequences in the Law of Attraction

How to Experience the Law of Attraction

An overview on the Laws of Attraction

The Law of Attraction and Relationships

Laws of Attraction in the Matter of Appearance

How to Practice the Laws of Attraction

The Law of Attraction In Action

The Law of Attraction In Business

The Law of Attraction: Does It Work?

The Law of Attraction And Physics

The Law of Attraction: Think Positive

The Law of Attraction In An Emergency Situation

The Law of Attraction Semantics

The Law of Attraction: Lose Weight

The Law of Attraction And Parenting

The Law of Attraction And "The Secret"

How To Attract Anything You Want In Life

The Law of Attraction Can Build Your Business

There are times when things seem unexpectedly to come our way. There will be an unexpected phone call or visit that will set things in motion. We have all heard of people who succeeded simply because they always seem to be in the right place at the right time. There are many words that are used in order to explain such happenings. Words like coincidence, serendipity, fate, luck, karma. Sayings like, "what goes around comes around" and so on. All of these words and expressions are different ways of summing up what is known as the Law of Attraction.

The Law of Attraction is very simply defined as that which attracts towards your life anything that you pay attention to, focus on, or spend energy on, whether you actually want it or not. You can use the Law of Attraction to build your business. The principles of the Law of Attraction can get you more clients, contracts, referrals, business partners, and of course money.

The first thing you need to know is how people use Declarative Statements and how they affect the Law of Attraction. A Declarative Statement is basically a positive expression targeted to that which you wish to attract. Such a statement leads to better feelings and moods. There are many forms of Declarative Statements and some of them may sound very egoistic in nature but that is how the whole thing works. If you are shy of being confident then you will have trouble working through the Law of Attraction.

Most of the time, failure in people is basically a subconscious acceptance of negative Declarative Statements. For example, saying things like, "My money always goes out faster than it comes in", or, "Business is good only around special occasions," are negative statements. Anything that makes you feel bad or say something negative about yourself or your business is a negative Declarative Statement.

The Law of Attraction will attract anything that you pay attention to. Stick to the positive and you will attract the positive. Keep thinking about the negative and that is all you will attract. The Law of Attraction does not care whether you want something or not or whether it will be good for you or not. It simple takes your current mood or feeling and goes ahead with it.

Every time you think something negative you should immediately dismiss it from your mind and rethink something positive. You will note and immediate improvement in your mood and feeling.

How To Attract Anything You Want In Life

Every time you make a negative Declarative Statement as yourself, "What do I want?" Focus on that aspect and rethink your thoughts. Once you know what you want you also know if it is good for you or not and you are bound to choose only that which is good.

You must practice on this until it becomes a habit so that you never have any negative thoughts. After a few days you will see that merely thinking positive will start making a healthy affect on your life and business.

How To Attract Anything You Want In Life

The Law of Attraction And Home Based Business

The Law of Attraction has been around for many years now. Though it was always quite popular among the self-help seekers and practitioners it is only recently that it has gathered worldwide attention as a major factor that influences our lives both personal and professional. The Law of Attraction has been discussed in detail by many prominent personalities and has found its way into many shows.

The Law of Attraction has a very simple definition that goes, "like attracts like". What the Law of Attraction states is that if you can think of it then you can achieve it. Human history is full of examples that prove this statement to be true. For example someone had to think that humans could fly in heavier-than-air planes.

Someone had to think up the steam engine. Someone had to picture a motorized carriage that would not need horses. All our progress in agricultures, technology, and the various branches of science is proof positive that human beings have the gift of realizing their dreams and making their imaginations come true. Thus we go from the horse to the car to the plane and faster than sound travel. All of this because someone thought that there has to be a faster way to travel.

The same Law of Attraction also applies to home based business. As mentioned earlier the Law of Attraction states that like attracts like. So if you firmly believe that you can succeed at home based business then you are bound to attract everything that will help you achieve that goal. As long as you are patient, persevering, and are completely committed and confident in your own success then there is no reason why you will not.

Success is often seen as something hard to achieve but this is simply because most people are already tuned into failure. An attitude like, "this will never work" or "I cannot do this" automatically predisposes them to failure even before they start. The successful people do not bother thinking about whether something will work or if they can do something or not. They approach everything positively. If this does not work then something else will but until it has stopped working they remain confident in the fact that they are doing the right thing. When you focus on the positive you attract more positivity towards yourself. This means that everyone around you will also share in your positive outlook and thereby the chances of success improve immediately.

How To Attract Anything You Want In Life

Most often people start a home business to pay off some bills, to get rid of their boss, to set their own hours, and so on. There is clarity in their thoughts about what they really want and this leads to failure because ambiguity leads to confusion. You must ask yourself what you really want and be clear that what you want is not a substitute for something else. If you started a home business for more money then how much money you want to make? Just to pay off some bills, fund your education, pay off the mortgage, or to get seriously rich?

You must be clear in your goals if you are to achieve them.

How To Attract Anything You Want In Life

The Law of Attraction And Getting Clients

Running your own business can often lead to problems like not having enough clients to stay afloat. This can lead to stress and worries about finances and the chances of surviving another year without going into debt. If you are currently in such a position then it may be a good idea for you to read about the Law of Attraction and how it can help you to shift your position to a better one.

The first thing to do is the stop worrying. Yes, you have probably heard of it many times. People are always saying that you should not worry but worry seems to find you on its own. The thing is that worry is not going to bring you what you need. What you need to do is focus on what you want rather than worry about is not being with you already. You must keep yourself open to receiving what you want. Thinking negatively closes the doors and brings in more negativity. So if you keep worrying about not having enough clients you will lose more clients. Instead be happy with the ones you have and stay positive that you will have more clients soon, without any doubt.

Sometimes people are not clear on what they really want. For example, if you are worrying you do not have enough clients then do you want more clients or are clients merely a bridge to what you really want, like money for instance. Your conscious and unconscious minds work differently. The thinking mind would naturally equate more clients with more money but the subconscious is only concerned with money. You cannot think clearly until both your minds are working in sync.

This means that you must focus on what you really want instead of what you think will fix the problem. Until you are completely clear in your mind what you want you will never achieve the kind of success that makes you envious. It may be only the slightest shift in how you think and you will be alright. The more clearly you focus on your goals consciously and subconsciously the better you are prepared to achieve them.

You must focus on everything positive and make it a habit not to dwell on the negative. Always keep in mind how you wish your life to be instead of complaining about how it is. The Law of Attraction will attract whatever you focus on. Focus on the negative and you will get only negativity. Focus on good things and good things will be attracted to you.

How To Attract Anything You Want In Life

Often times you will be told to be practical. While this advice makes a lot of sense it is sometimes not entirely true. The human instinct is a powerful tool. If you deeply feel that you ought to do something then you should do it provided it is positive. Do not deprive yourself of your instinct to prove you are practical. It is important to relax and let your thinking mind take a break while you follow your feelings every once in a while.

How To Attract Anything You Want In Life

The Law of Attraction And Network Marketing

The Law of Attraction can make a huge and positive impact on your personal life as well as professional future. One of the biggest growing fields of business is network marketing and nothing can help you create a network faster and better than the Law of Attraction.

There are many excellent examples of how the Law of Attraction has been used by individuals to better their personal and professional status. The Law of Attraction can bring success in business and also lead to better and stronger personal relationships with clients and intimates. Despite all this there are very few people who actually bother to find out what the Law of Attraction can do for them. Not only does the law affect the goal but it also has a positive impact on the path taken to reach the goal.

The Law of Attraction is based on the principle that like attracts like. This simply means that the more positive you think the more positivity you will attract. Thinking of success will lead to success and pondering or worrying about failure will only bring more failure. Even in moments of failure or negativity it is crucial to stay focused on the positive and not give in to negativity. The Law of Attraction is blind in the sense that it simply takes your thoughts and feelings and brings about more of the same. By staying positive you are forcing the Law of Attraction to bring you good things. If you want something then do not think of what will happen if you do not get it. That is futile. Instead focus on all the good things that will happen once you do get it. The more positive you think the closer you will be to achieving whatever you desire. All you need to do is apply this to network marketing and you too can become a powerful networker.

As stated earlier, the most important thing is to stay positive. Thinking positive will attract more positivity.

This positive feeling will in turn define your actions that will eventually lead to a positive outcome. Once you are doing this constantly it will be noticed by everyone you meet and you will have no trouble passing on your positivity and passion to others. The more you can ignite them with your own fervor the better and bigger your network will become. Remember that people are more willing to spend money on something that excites and interests them and makes them feel good. Share your positivity and they will readily become part of your network.

How To Attract Anything You Want In Life

The next thing is to be clear on your goals and what exactly you want. Do not be ambiguous otherwise you will only get more ambiguity in return. Visualization is the key to realizing your goals. You must be able to see yourself succeeding in your mind. Write down about your success and read it to yourself. This makes things real because humans do not read in words but think in pictures what they read

How To Attract Anything You Want In Life

The Law of Attraction In Sales And Marketing

The Law of Attraction is one of the most popular areas of personal development today. The Law of Attraction is very simple stated as follows: You will attract towards you whatever you focus on. What this means is that what you think of most is likely to represent your reality in the future. So if you keep thinking of yourself as successful and happy then your life will automatically steer itself in that direction. If you keep too much negativity inside you then you will attract only more of the same. In other words, a positive mindset will help you achieve what you want and a negative attitude will only multiply your failure. The more strongly you believe in yourself and your own happiness and success the more you focus on all the good things that can happen to you and the more you cut out all negative thoughts out of your life the better you will live.

It is important to understand how the Law of Attraction affects people in sales and marketing.

The Law of Attraction says that you will receive what you give. When you are making a sale you must focus on giving the clients more than what they expect. If you focus on closing the sale then that is all you will achieve. Instead think of building a relationship, be positive and infuse your clients with your positivity. Make them think like you think about what you are selling.

A lot depends on the "unique selling point" of your product so keep you USPs handy. If you are good at something then use it to distinguish yourself from your competitors. If something makes you unique then you can use that as your USP. If you have received compliments from your clients then think about what brought forward those compliments. Did they say they found you cheerful, friendly, reliable, easy to talk to, or something else? Make the list and work on it. You will discover that they are your customers not because of your product but because of you. Working on what makes you unique is also a good way to build confidence. The more people like you the more you will like yourself and that will increase the positivity you radiate. Your clients will subconsciously feel that positive attitude and will respond positively to whatever you say.

Do not set limits on yourself. Most failure comes from acknowledging some lack in yourself. Do not hold back because you think you cannot do something. The simply approach is to just do the thing and watch the results.

How To Attract Anything You Want In Life

Sometimes you will have this nagging feeling that the only answer you are going to get is "no". Take a hint from telemarketers, they never let any number of negative responses stop them, they just keep going.

You must believe that your clients like talking to you. This can only happen if you work on how they can benefit every time they speak to you. Remember that it is not all about making a sale. Above all else you must always approach your clients with the attitude that they will do something positive for you.

How To Attract Anything You Want In Life

Laws of Attraction - The Alpha Male Mentality

Interactions between the males species has always been with the survival philosophy of "survival of the fittest." The male that survives is chosen based on strong breed This is especially true in animal pack societies, in which the alpha male would be the only one among the pack. His job would be to get all the females pregnant so the species could continue to live.

Alpha males in the Animal Kingdom

The male human species look upon this situation strangely with a hint of pensiveness. what would it be like to be the top king of the gang? To be the one who procreates to survive. However, those males do not understand that the alpha male becomes this title not by a birthright but by proving time and again that he is the strongest and the most intelligent to survive. Yet, should another male challenge the alpha male to a duel, then the alpha male must fight in order to keep his back. Should he decline, it will be removed from him. This is to ensure that the species indeed continue to exist because the alpha male is likely to rear strong children.

This is good for the animal kingdom but what does this do for the human race. How do the two relate. In fact, there are alpha males in the human race. Yet the criteria for these alpha males are set differently than those in the animal kingdom. These are five categories of alphas in the human race. They are: the powerful alpha, intellectual alpha, military alpha, bad boy alpha and the artistic alpha

Definitions of the Four Alpha Males -

In the powerful alpha, it is the man who has the greatest and most power. This holds true with their community, family and friends as well as their business. Women who are engrossed to this type of alpha are looking at business tycoons, politicians and possibly even royalty. It's because woman want these positions and the power that the position brings to it.

Intellectual Alpha - Men who are smart on any topics or subjects. These men are likely to go through school to get their PhDs and are likely to save the world. Where these males can be found in their offices and work places along with their counterparts...their mates.

How To Attract Anything You Want In Life

Military alpha - these are the men women tend to love. Women love men in uniform because they have "power", have an adventurous sense as well as a job that can be brought and talked about although the phrase, "that's classified" would be a mood killer. Their mates know that the military alpha will be out of country a good part of the time so bonding is never very big.

The bad boy alpha can take on many forms. He can be of military Special Forces or with black ops. He can have a dappled past and one criminal element that may have a price on his head. He may not strike about conversations and talk a lot but he assumes the woman he is with will know what he wants or needs.

The artistic alpha would be the type to sell drawings in museums but have his showings somewhere exotic. This type of male is of the romantic side and women will be adorned by this alpha.

Do the males you know fit into one of these five categories? Every woman has wanted to date at least one of them. As the military marines' saying goes, "the few, the proud, we're the alpha males.

How To Attract Anything You Want In Life

Law Of Attraction - Study Of How Different Cultures React On Dating

When a person attracts the attention of the one that have an interest in, it's only half the battle. Now that this interest has been piqued, where do you go from here?

Since the world is one big melting pot with the many different cultures in it, it is not simple to ask the love of your life or rather that affection that melts your heart and keeps you sane, for supper and drinks. There are many different rules on dating since there are many diverse cultures. While asking someone out could be simple, this often times not the case because any violations of differing cultures can make you a person of distaste and be ridiculed in the eyes of the one person who you wish to impress most.

Many, if not most, individuals comprehend that not all the societies have identical views on relationships between a man and a woman. This means typically any minor infractions in the relationship are bound to go unnoticed. Yet, it is still important to understand the guidelines in your mate's culture. The people of the United States have, to a great extent, looser view on dating positions than those held by other countries.

America's view on Dating

In America, physical touching is allowed on the very first date...although only hand holding and kissing at the end of the night is expected so long as both parties are interested in doing so. Should this not be the case of both parties, then the date would be long, boring and rather uneventful.

Eastern World views on dating

In the Eastern and Asian countries, including Korea and Japan, dating may be allowed but unlike Americans, public shows of affection and physical interaction are scowled at. In many cases, kissing and hand holding may not be at ease for the folks of this area. This is especially true if they are in front of strangers.

How To Attract Anything You Want In Life

In other parts of the world, dating is not done at all. In fact, it is discouraged. Should a man and woman like each other, it is anticipated that their ultimate solution or goal would be to get married. Every step should be done with marriage being the ultimate realization of the goal.

Arranged marriages in other cultures

Yet, there are still several cultures where members determine who will date who from another family. It is under the assumption that who they choose will take the time to get to know the other and will join in on family events. Doing otherwise is thought of as rude and insulting. In other cultures though, joining on the family gatherings should not be done until marriage is established.

There is no doubt, there are pitfalls when trying to form a bond across cultural dividers. If a person wants to date someone outside their culture, they should take the time to study how the person's courtship works. This is to avoid any issues that could arise.

How To Attract Anything You Want In Life

The Law of Attraction and Your Body

Financial freedom? This is a success many people try to obtain. For many people, the Law of Attraction has worked for them. It has also helped them obtain fuller lives through enhanced affairs. This law, the Law of Attraction, can indeed have an effect of the body.

First, think of how this law works. Whether you realize it or not, the human body is made up of energy that is either positive or negative. This factor depends on whether the person wants to think more on the positive aspect s of life or the negative ones. Life is made up of both good and bad experiences, which make us grow.

These good and bad factors affect not only the person it happens to but others as well. Should you want only positive energy, then focusing only on the good aspects on life is what you need to do. A good way to use this Law of Attraction process is by visualization.

Competitors employ a technique called Visual Motor Rehearsal to see what potential actions will hold. This practice is a Law of Attraction. Let's take the example of hooking them up to a monitor and have them practice the event on their mind. It would show that the athlete's muscles obeying their thoughts although the muscles weren't being actively used. When the actual competition occurred, the athletes are much prepared for the event as if they were doing the practicing all along. This is a form of Law of Attraction.

With this type of law, being able to feel the realism of plans and imaginings coming true is pretty nice. Using visualization during the Law of Attraction, it can help with any physical task you will begin or undertake.

Should you be thinking about climbing Mt. Fuji, using the Law of Attraction to see it occurring and then believing it, makes you think it can happen. Positive feelings envelop the person about the accomplishment about to be taken and then it comes back to you as positive energy.

It can also be used for healing. Medicine, when needed, should be used. It thought that by using the Law of Attraction, that medication can be facilitated greatly when it is used with positive energy or positive thoughts.

How To Attract Anything You Want In Life

Remember the placebo effect? That health or behavior improvement is not attributed to medicine or treatment. That should prove that positive thinking does have an effect on one's well being. If a person feels good about medicine they have to take, the more likely they are to be healed by said medication. This occurs even when the medicine is a sugar pill or a scientific formula used to cure or aid illnesses.

Not to say that some diseases need medicine and treatments. It is these people who need medication to survive a disease or live with a disease that often times get depressed or even discouraged. So long as these folks remain positive and have a positive outlook, then there is an improved likelihood of survival.

Half of using this Law of Attraction is seeing in the mind the course of being well. If you come to believe you are getting better, than it will be so. Remember to try and dwell on the happy or positive side of life and surround yourself with positive thinking and a positive atmosphere. Be around things you enjoy thus keeping up the focus of positive energy.

How To Attract Anything You Want In Life

Law Of Attraction - Raising Your Attraction Potential

It is clear what the law of attraction is all about: to choice a mate best suited by their skill to endure although it is not their only factor when determining the human match. It leaves great deal for leeway for those people have not found the niche with associates of the opposite sex. Yet there are five techniques that can be used to exponentially increase the impending attraction.

Attraction tip #1 - Dressing for Success - It is easy to forget that over the lessons of the day, the way a person presents themselves will determine how others' opinions of them will help or hinder in finding a mate.. It is important that people take pride in themselves. Remember the old saying... first impressions are everything. There is no second chance to make an impression. A person forms their opinion of you based on how you look, not what matters on the inside. Select attire that are relaxed but fit you well and in style plus colors that are gratifying to the person. Anyone can create an optimistic feeling to those of the opposite sex.

If you feel like you need a little help in this area, a sales clerk at a retail-clothing store can help in selecting clothing that is just right for a person. Many have been in the industry for a long time so they are pleased to lend their experience in putting their customers in clothing that suits them and putting their foot in the doorway of attraction. This also helps them in getting customers to return to their shop.

Attraction Tip #2 - Get a Hobby - With today's busy lifestyle, most of it revolving around work. Not many people have a hobby anymore, with them focusing all their time on work. Work does not give us an enormous deal of time to talk with other people. But getting a hobby increases those chances dramatically. It shows others that you have something other than work in your life. You don't want to be remembered as a workaholic.

Attraction Tip #3 - Keep Up on Current Events - This provides excellent communication interaction between people. You can be in a group and know what people are talking about if you keep up on the current events. You do not want to be the only one not chiming in on the important details.

How To Attract Anything You Want In Life

Attraction Tip #4 - Smile - If you are smiling it means you are self confident and do not mind if opposite sex members cone to meet you or you them. It doesn't mean you aren't shy, but you are confident in yourself. Smiling will naturally get people curious about whom you are and ask questions.

Attraction Tip #5 - Find unknown but not uncomfortable situations - This can serve as two parts for the attraction. It opens a person to situations that normally felt weird to be in and gets the person to meet other people. Having someone show the ropes of your present area shows in a helpful way your willingness to adapt.

Using the tricks of the trade means you won't be alone for long. Do not expect results right away because beauty is not only skin deep, it is also on the outside. You must have a wonderful personality to match the beauty to the outside

How To Attract Anything You Want In Life

Some Fascinating Books On The Law Of Attraction

It seems that the "Law of Attraction" had concepts that have been around for centuries with several authors exploring the concepts and writing about them. Currently, many books on the "law of Attraction" have been written. Discussed below are the more prominent and featured books published.

Hicks' Law of Attraction

Ester and Jerry Hicks wrote a book simply named "Law of Attraction". The two were inspired by what they call is a spirit who tells them that they need to instruct people to getting by they want just by believing. The book Law of Attraction is based on the practicalities and the principles of the Law of Attraction. If you read the book, you should have a greater understanding of how things turn out to be. It is then you will understand that the role you play is making the events around you too.

However, this book is not for everyone due to the religious theme it has in it. Yet, if you want to see how the Law of Attraction is applied, this is a good back to read.

Both Ester and Jerry Hicks have written several books on this law. One book is called "The Amazing Power of Deliberant Intent." The book is finding and having about balance in your life. The concept Emotional Guidance System is used in this book to explain on how keeping your life on track while using the Law of Attraction.

One early book entitled "Ask and It is Given" and is a practical exercise in creating and achieving the life you want. The book has a 22-step process outlined that helps you use the law that will help you along the way.

Byrne Law Of Attraction Book

Author Rhonda Byrne also wrote a book on the law of attraction. She centered her book on the knowledge of the principles being handed down over time. The book focuses on certain people, past and present.

How To Attract Anything You Want In Life

Those involved it the current thinking of Law of Attraction argue about how its progression works. Those people advise why it works and what it has done for their lives, good and bad.

Losier's newer book on the Law of Attraction

Michael J. Losier currently had a new book published about the law. Its title is "Law of Attraction: The Science of Attracting More of What You Want and Less of What You Don't Want." He talks quite a bit about positive and negative vibrations. The book is laid out in a step by step format.

Taylor focuses on Law of Attraction

Another author named Sandra Anne Taylor discusses how the law can work in the aspect of the love life. Her book is titled, "Secrets of Attraction: The Universal Law of Love, Sex and Romance." She stresses how love is not a feeling but rather energy. She talks about of personal energy fields which affect the way people will perceive or see someone. This field, she said, changes or influences how people act when they are around other people. The principle behind the thought was to change how the energy is around people; in turn, changing the person's love life too.

There are still numerous books out on the topic of Law of Attraction. By going to the library and looking them up or finding them on the Internet, maybe on Amazon.com or other bookstore sites. Reading these books could change your life.

How To Attract Anything You Want In Life

The Law Of Attraction

Certainly by now you have heard of the Law of Attraction even if you aren't that interested in new age ideas. The theory behind the whole idea is people can have the desire they wish for as long as they think very long and hard about it. All up to the point where they can feel it and see it although it is not there yet. It must be said though even if you develop into what you like, you take the bad with the good.

Whether you like it or whether you don't, the Law of Attraction will work. It has always been that way and it will always be the way it is until there is no more wishing, praying, feelings or beliefs, than the idea will survive. Everything you do leaves a spot in space and the same goes with our feelings and our wishes. The Law of Attraction does exist just like the sun rises in the east and sets in the west. Some people consider thing that cannot be proved or have an explanation behind it is considered faith or miracles or even something that was meant to happen. This Law of Attraction studies behind the "it was meant to happen belief."

This Law of Attraction will bound to teach you that should you think of something that you want positively, it will occur. Yet, if you think negatively, then bad things are bound to happen. Although bad things can happen that aren't bound to the law though most of the time it is. Case in point... you are scared that you be robbed when you are walking. This thought is every day. Eventually one day this will be the actual case.

But there are cases where the regulation cannot apply. For example, a baby/toddler who has been abused cannot begin to understand what is happening to them and do not have the capability to say, I wish this would happen to me.

Think for a moment about your setting as a comic strip that is created every time you flip the pages in the book. This means you, your own being and self, is responsible for the environment that has been created around you. You are the one holding the strings while the people and the events surrounding you are your puppets. Is this the way you anticipated your life? Just change the way it turns out, if it is not the way you want things to be.
Every being has the ability to change what they do not like about their surroundings. No one can create it for you, so you need to do it for yourself if you do not like it. Course there those that wanted something to occur to you despite your not wanting it to. It does not mean you did

How To Attract Anything You Want In Life

anything wrong or could not change it to your advantage, it was just not to be the way you wanted it.

So when it's time to get out of your boring lifestyle since you no longer care for it, only pure positive thinking is the way to go. By changing your lifestyle and your way of thinking can you truly be living your reverie. Do not forget your brain, it is a great tool to use with our abilities.

How To Attract Anything You Want In Life

Law Of Attraction - How The Human Race Chooses Their Mates

The procedure of deciding a mate is not done entirely on physical traits: their strengths, their courage and their ability to hunt and provide for the family. It is those principles that can be applied to many cases in the human world. Yet, since our minds are much more urbanized than those of the animal kingdom, we, as humans, do take other things into account when choosing our lifetime mates.

While the practice of mate choosing is based upon the ability to provide is a very important thing, the capacity in the human world is not to be judged in the capability to go out hunting and for wild animals, it is based on the ability to meet all their responsibilities that the female counterpart expects. The expectations of your future should persuade you in the amount of accountability your mate has. If you wish to retire at an early age, then you need a mate who is willing to work and forfeit for the goal not someone who wants to goof off and work until they die.

However, if you wish to establish a family right off, then you need to prefer a mate who is keen to carry out their part in the home responsibility and put future job advancements on hold. Children are a necessary responsibility and one person should not handle it alone. Should you be a free spirit, then finding a free spirit such as yourself is priority number one. You need to find someone who has the same viewpoints as yourself. Whatever the situation, you need to find a mate who is willing to hold up their end of the deal when it comes to your future together. Should you find a mate that is unwilling to decide their path can be fine in the beginning, the strain it puts on the relationship can kill it altogether especially if the worry is on the financial end.

Another thing to consider is common interest. Opposites do attract sometimes but it is better to have a mate who has many key standards and interests in common than those that do not. It is likely the relationship would have a superior chance of surviving that way. It does not mean you need to have an identical twin in this case because if there were no difference, what would be there to talk about? While you need to have some of the same activities, there does not need to be a stalemate in the relationship either. Do not forget that a common picture of the future is important. A common path is needed because while attraction is fine in the very beginning, in the end it is going to fail if the male and female do not agree on the future of what they want.

How To Attract Anything You Want In Life

This choosing of a mate should not be lightly done. An incorrect chose can lead to melancholy for all parties concerned. Carefully review your chose in mates and decide who would be better for you in the long term.

How To Attract Anything You Want In Life

How To Compete With The Alpha Male

Throughout the years, the female of any group is fascinated by an alpha male that she hopes will let her bear his offspring - where the offspring have an opportunity to survive in the big, bad world that they will be brought into and raised in. These females are not in the hunt for a relationship that is meaningful and long-term. All they are looking for is quick interlude then have the privilege of bearing a child. The alpha male, is lucky in this regard, since he has a gang and while he must protect them all, he does not provide them all individual attention of himself.

This does ring true to the alpha male human. The alpha male is extremely loyal to those people he chooses to defend and will go out of his way to not hurt them; but he was also not give them his heart. A female of captures and pins down the alpha male is truly a rare woman. Since there are many other "fish in the sea" who are seeking more than what the alpha male can offer, it would be indeed these fishes that will defeat the alpha male's grasp on the female he has chosen to set his sights upon.

A non-alpha male must remember that when he goes into a relationship, he needs to be going in as if he is looking for an everlasting mate but not expecting one either. This means do not propose on the second date, no matter if the woman you want to propose to is the woman of your dreams. A woman who chooses to be with a non-alpha male will go into any relationship cautiously and eyes wide open. She will look to see what the man she has chosen has to offer. He will need to provide her with a sheltered financial future (this can easily be done by going to college and setting a realistic ten-year plan in your twenties.) She will also look for emotional security that she would be lacking in the alpha male. The man who is not an alpha male should not be with a woman if he feels he cannot give himself to a situation that is going to matter. He will need to keep things light and be friends with the female that way he would not get a bad reputation with female acquaintances.

Remember if you are not an alpha male, you may have to fight to get where you want. While you are without the advantage, you do have resources at your disposal. Take advantage of a situation where the female sees you at your best, if it is possible. If not, try to establish that. Women love confident men.

Things not to do:
* Stutter

How To Attract Anything You Want In Life

* Drool
* Spill Your Drink
* Say anything that resembles a pick-up or come-on line

Things to do:
* Smile (naturally of course)
* Talk in the normal tone of voice
* Look at her in the eye
* Start the conversation. (If this seems to be a problem, pick out something in your environment that you find yourself in.)
* Walk her to her car at the end of the night
* Ger her phone number
* Most importantly, call her!

Following these guidelines and allowing a relationship to grow between you and your female counterpart can be based on common interest and respect. Before you know it, she can look at you and say "Alpha who?"

How To Attract Anything You Want In Life

Scientific Study Of Male And Female Interactions

What is it behind the attraction for men to women and women to men? What is it about the individual that makes them irresistible to their opposite counterpart? There is a number of factors that needs to be considered; yet let's look at the core of the predicament: the Science of Attraction.

The main component that allows for mate selection seems to lie in the evolutionary need for the species to continue. There is no doubt that in animal species, the strong is chosen to carry on the reproduction process because it is likely they would produce strong or stronger offspring. Weak members are never chosen in the animal kingdom because of the need to survive. If weak members were chosen to procreate, it is likely their children would be weak as well, possibly not surviving into adulthood thus this would end the species.

Primarily, males and females that battled and proved themselves strongest attracted mates more often. Then, they would choose from the strongest from those. Mother Nature's circle of life would indeed go on, with genes often ensuring their children were given ample opportunity in the very beginning of their lives. No different from males and females of the human race search out those people of the healthiest and physically fit types. It is they who can survive physically in the environment.

Set aside those of strongest and survivalist, pheromones play a big part in attracting mates. What are pheromones? Pheromones are chemically secreted molecules that are produced and carried through an airborne route, which causes a great deal of sexual response in animals (including humans, too.) An animal carries the belief that the pheromone allowed the animal to choose a mate based up its ability to produce offspring with a strong immune system.

Up until recently, it was thought the human race had lost the pheromone ability to attract a mate. However, research into how much of a role pheromones play on the human race is not available. All of it is in the matter of speculation. So with this being the case, is the human race no different from their animal kingdom when it comes to avoiding extinction

It all seems that scientific evidence pertaining to the human attraction to one another lies in the ability to produce strong children. It seems that pheromones offer the child the greatest possible

How To Attract Anything You Want In Life

combinations of immune systems that will ensure their well being. A physical attraction guarantees the child will have the physically best chance to survive in their adulthood. All this supports the theory of survival of the fittest.

How To Attract Anything You Want In Life

The Consequences In The Law Of Attraction

Every adult knows that when you have an action, you end up with a reaction. With every move we make, we end up with some kind of consequence. However, adults need to teach children that everything has a consequence.

Yet, not all consequences are bad. A good consequence is flowers growing when it rains and then the sun comes out. This is a positive consequence.

However, a negative consequence can be when a person is out in public drinking alcohol and then gets behind the wheel of a car and driving it. This can come with a very high price... either with an accident or getting caught by police and going to jail.

This holds true when you talk about the law of attraction. If a person follows the law, then it is supposed to lead to gratification and maybe even happiness. But there is always a price to pay when you break the law.

Only when you break this law, it is not as simple as going to jail or doing community service. This breakage of the law will follow you for the reminder of your life. Some of the law breaking-negative consequence is listed below.

* You will grow old, perhaps fat, bald and alone
* You could have a Hell's Angel gang after you for the rest of your life
* You'll find yourself married, raising a family and living in a small town, all after you get married after only two dates.
* You'll be unemployed
* You'll be in jail
* You may have an unhappy wife or husband stalking you
* You could be the king or queen of a barren island
* You may tell tales of your humiliation to family and friends
* You won't be invited to Happy Hour on Fridays anymore
* No more office party invitations
* You could be sleeping in the barn rather than a house
* Your pride could be broken where you walk with your head in shame and not up high

How To Attract Anything You Want In Life

* You can never look your friends in the eye again
* Old friends will never be friends of the future as it is just too weird
* You could be in love with someone but never get the feeling returned
* Strange men and women will be calling your home all the time, at all hours
* Strange packages will be on your doorstep every day
* Your kids could end up hating you
and
* You could be at the business end of a pink slip or a gun.

Of course, these are extreme situations where you may or may not find yourself at. Although the possibility does exist, one wrong step does not mean all bad things will happen to you from that point on.

It is imperative that people weight their choices carefully when it comes to things of importance. For your see... the law of attraction can go either way: it is either a positive or negative consequences.

How To Attract Anything You Want In Life

How To Experience The Law Of Attraction

The Law of Attraction - it's a recent concept that the scientific community is finally acknowledging that exists. Yet, most of society does not see it that way since it is fairly new. So how do we get one see that the Law of Attraction is real? How can we convince one person to see that what you want and what you get are two separate things?

The Power of Wishing & the Law of Attraction

The first thing to do is to imagine something you terribly want. Something you know could not ever happen. Imagine yourself with what you want, touching it and feeling it. Then should everything go well and the way you want, then your dreams should come true.

Despite the power of wishing, you need to be realistic. Case in point with wanting dessert after supper, just because you wish you could have dessert after your supper, does not always make it so.

Society nowadays is a lot more cautious especially with fraud cases becoming more and more frequent and people being more aware of them. No wonder it is getting harder and harder to prove that the Law of Attraction is what the person experienced.

Law of Attraction tests

How can we test the Law of Attraction so it is easy to understand? Let us try this experiment. It is simple and require things easily found in a household. Take a small bit of carpet and a glass of grape juice. Can you see where this is heading? The idea is to fill a glass full of grape juice...indeed to the very tip and walk across the "white" carpet without spilling a single drop.

If you do not happen to have carpeting, then it would be irrelevant to try the experiment. There is another people can try. Even if you have never played golf, try playing it for this idea. Find a hole that already has water in it. The idea is to hit the ball over the danger. Imagine the ball going over the hole as you hit the ball with the golf club. What was the end result? Did your ball go into the water?

How To Attract Anything You Want In Life

If you decided to do the two experiments and it did not go the way you wanted, then you were probably asking for it. You, more than likely, thought in the back of your mind about not spilling the glass of grape juice or doing a good golf shot. These were only two things in the mass of other signals we do not think of because they happen often. Imagine all the things we miss just because of this oversight?

Remember, the Law of Attraction is giving us what we asked for. In both of these "examples", they fell into the negative side instead of the positive one because a bad result came out in each one.

If one person is convinced about the Law of Attraction being real, then that is one less person to convince and one more to convince others. If you understand the Law of Attraction, then you might be on your way to create a more happier lifestyle. If not though, then it means it will only be faith, nothing more. Yet, most scientists understand it is the law that something does happen.

How To Attract Anything You Want In Life

An Overview On The Laws Of Attraction

For every game played in life it does have its rules. Soccer - you cannot use your hands. Poker - you can't look at your opponents' hand. Scrabble - no looking in the dictionary trying to find words to use. Each rule set forth is considered as if it were set in stone. However, rules do have conditions that can be broken.

It should be said that the game of dating is done an identical ways. To capture that interest of the person you so desire, there are certain guidelines that you must follow. On top of that, there are rules for once you captures set person's attention. These rules may seem iron clad but again, rules were meant to be broken. It is bad when a man is not proverbial with these rules regarding the Laws of Attraction since a violation of them can lead them to loneliness, shame and despair. Not all rules are written down for the viewing public; some are just general common sense knowledge, others are known by the individual themselves. Those who try and enter the scene will need to be educated on each of the games' rules before they decide they want anything more to do with that person.

The Laws of Attraction are founded on supply and demand. When there are plenty of mates (fish in the sea) available, then an individual, based up the supply and demand, is allowed to be picky and choosy on what they want from a person. Should there be a low mate supply, the demand is going to be high and the law allows for more leeway. If a mate cannot be found than the species would eventually become extinct. This becomes the last man on earth philosophy. Be assured should you be the last man on earth, any woman would be glad to have you.

The supply and demand theory is seen throughout every bit of life. One area do not have exclusively. It can be seen in the animal and insect kingdom, among birds, fish and bees. Every species has a meticulous set of rules it adheres to when they judge their mate and rules to those exceptions.

For the animal kingdom it is a general need of mates, as is understood by the supply and demand theory. In the human species, there is the majority of Earth's surface that bend for the laws of human attraction, which are not so stringent, that require the abolition of the species.

How To Attract Anything You Want In Life

The other series of articles that follows will touch on an assortment of laws of attraction and how to get around them. Each article can stand alone for those who wish to join in the core but the articles together serve as a guide to circumvent even the most complex conditions to attract the ideal mate.

How To Attract Anything You Want In Life

The Law Of Attraction And Relationships

It has been believed many times that the Laws of Attraction can patent itself when it comes to the matters of wealth, happiness and health. Having a meaningful relationship is part of the pleasure that is felt. The relationships can be of love, family or even simple relationships. The Laws of Attraction affect each one of them.

Whether you are knowingly using the Laws of Attraction in your life, it is always working in your life. A person is always placing vibrations out in the universe thus collecting like energies that will and do come back to them.

It is when you intentionally use the Laws of Attraction that you must focus on what you fancy. Afterward, these encouraging items arrive to you. What becomes important is what you put your attention to the most and when you put all importance into that one thing, you begin to get excited about it. The excitement turns into a greater power than any drummed up by simply saying again and again what you are wanting. This Law of Attraction works the same way in relations as well.

The Law of Attraction can help people find that one person most special to them and bring the mate to the person through this law. You need to first determine what type of mate you want. Make a list if need be and write down your strengths and the strengths that you are looking for. Also, write down the joys you would love to share with your special someone.

Once you have that more concrete list and idea of what you are looking for then the universe, according to the Law of Attraction, will bring you the mate you have been waiting for. Of course, all this will ensue through a series of frequencies. You send out what you want, that pulsation goes out and gathers other frequencies you may like. In other simple terms, your matches.

It is usually a matter of moments before two people meet because their frequencies were vibrating at the same time. Thus the Law of Attraction is at work. Always follow your instincts and if you have the urge to do something else on a whim, do it. It could be on your meet your perfect mate.

How To Attract Anything You Want In Life

Letting the Law of Attraction do the work is best in this case. Repeatedly to confirm in your mind that the person you are seeking for does, in fact, exist. You must remember to believe in that person. If you draw attention and overall excitement to it, then things will happen. You have to believe it will.

In the theory of matching, it does work well with other relationships. If you put energy and time toward an individual in your life, then that energy can be for them or against them. This depends on the amount of power you send them and what type. In return, you will get a matched frequency and get the consequence you expected. This is called the Law of Attraction.

With the Law of Attraction, should you be feeling down, it will provide you with a person with an even despair. As you both fall down deeper into despair, then you will be deciding if the law is better working against you or for you and you will choose for you in most cases. Find ways to vibrate in positive efforts. You should be able to reinforce and elongate friendships like never before with this being the case.

How To Attract Anything You Want In Life

Laws Of Attraction In The Matter Of Appearance

Do you wake up, get a shower and wonder what you are going to wear? Do you spend more than an hour getting ready so you can look good when you go outside or are you one of these people who throw on whatever you can, not caring about the thoughts of others? Did you know that what you wear matters?

When others meet you for the very first time, how you appear to them tells them much about you. It also tells them if they want to be friends with you or move on. What you wear says many things about you and about who you desire to be?

Creating a positive initial impression with a clean and neat appearance is a very important part of meeting someone. Slobs do not attract people around them. It tells people that you have no desire for the regards of yourself or anyone else who you may come into contact with.

Remember that members of the opposite sex are attracted to those people who believe to be on top of "food chain". This is metaphorically speaking, of course. Course no one is going to think this way if you cannot do things for yourself without assistance.

Appearance of Clothing

Clothes should be clean, neat and properly fitting so the image you present to others is one as if you care about yourself as well as your belongings and the people around you. It is rare to care about yourself and not others around you but it is quite easy to care for others and not yourself.

This does not mean you should spend a fortune on clothing, jewelry, make-up and anything else that would make you spend more than what is necessary. Plus you do not need to spend more than three hours getting all spruced up. Let the essence of yourself shine through without getting overly done. Even when you look like that, it can tell people that you are trying to hard. Be yourself but look good doing it.

What kind of clothing should you wear? Ask for help.

How To Attract Anything You Want In Life

If you do not know what your essence...remember that for most people, wearing jeans and sweatshirts or t-shirts are comfortable, every-day clothing. Much more comfortable than wearing dress clothes. You must understand that just because you choose comfortably clothing over dress clothing, does not mean you care less about yourself and how you appear to others.

If you are hesitant about the taste of your clothing, there are people out there who can help you. People can go to sales clerk, especially those in retail clothing, who are qualified to have a good eye for what does and does not look good on people. Most people do not know what looks good on them even though they think it does. A common misconception which is why it is always good to have a friend go shopping with you. A second opinion is always best when buying clothing. With sales clerks, they know if they help their customers buy nice clothing, that the customer is likely to come back.

You must remember that a second impression never happens and that first impression is everything. If you make a negative impression from the get-go, it can be very damaging. Try to look your best even if you run out to get something from the grocery store. If you put your best foot forward, you are likely to be remembered for someone who takes pride in themselves.

How To Attract Anything You Want In Life

How To Practice The Laws Of Attraction

Try to imagine if you had all the money you might need and want and never have the need to want for it again. Next imagine if you had immense affairs with everyone you knew and are in a wonderful state of well being. Again, imagine you spending your life in perfect harmony and in complete peace. Should you carry out the Laws of Attraction, it is said you will get these things and more so long as you believe it will be so.

The first thing to do is to perform the Law of Attraction and embrace the feeling of appreciation. Be thankful and grateful for all that you have and center on only the superior things in life. Doing so will bring positive sentiments according to the law.

Now those positive feelings will turn themselves into positive energy, thus according to the Laws of Attraction it is supposed to be. It is when you send out the positive energy that you are to see good things return back to you through this law. For example, you are holding onto a luck charm, say for instance, a bent penny, by concentrating on those positive things it reminds you to be appreciative every time you touch it or see it.

Be aware of the thoughts you have according to the Laws of Attraction. Many people go through their days with flitting thoughts going in and out. Of course, many people pay little attention to this detail. Should you be conscious on the Laws of Attraction, then you can monitor them thoughts on a certain degree level. You can eventually get a feel for where your thoughts are headed. Do they lead down a negative path? If so, using the Laws of Attraction can change that.

You should, before much else, figure out what it is that you want. These things do not need to be things that are easy to get but rather things that can be attainable with a little bit of hard work. Going for your dreams shouldn't be a hard thing. Example: the universe will not give a different exertion to give you something fantastic in return. Thus the Laws of Attraction applies to supply them.

Perhaps you really don't know what you want. You have been told over and over again No, you can't have that that you pretty much have stopped wanting it. Yet, it is time to do some soul searching and find out what you could get through those Laws of Attraction that is going to please you. Go through magazines, head out to showroom floors and look at model houses.

How To Attract Anything You Want In Life

Who knows? Maybe some ideas will start popping out at you. Yet, the Laws of Attraction do not work this way. It works to remember that all you need is to trust that the good thing will happen and leave the rest up to the universe.

If you know the Laws of Attraction, it can alter your life. It takes certain mindsets to work within these laws but mastering it is never hard, even if it seems like it is. All you need is a bit of patience, time and above all else... faith.

How To Attract Anything You Want In Life

The Law of Attraction In Action

What would happen if you were suddenly bestowed with the power to bring in more happiness into your life?

Wouldn't it be great if you could get all that you have ever desired? In case you were told from an early age that too much desire is not good for your spiritual health, then you will be glad to know that it is logically an invalid statement. We exist because of desire. In addition, you can gain a lot by cultivating the simple power within yourself, merely by employing the laws of attraction.

Desire is what keeps us all alive. It is not to be misunderstood and shunned. You must understand that man is the most beautifully designed God's creations.

We human beings have the magic of creation within ourselves. You do not need a magic wand, a genie, or a magic potion to wield the beautiful magic within your soul!

In fact, the Holy Bible acknowledges the power of man when it says that we were created in "the image of God" and we always reap what we sow. Another line that you have surely heard is that God helps people who help themselves. In order to help ourselves, we have to realize our potential as divine beings and meditate towards attaining the level of focus and determination. A great way to do this is to create a positive feeling deep within our minds. One can do this by praying with a definite and positive bent of mind. All you have to do is visualize your desires and thank the almighty even before you attain what you desire. This will help create a bond between you and the Almighty. This will be a very effective prayer because through this you are showing your undivided faith in God. Thus, a prayer is answered best when you display unmoved faith in God.

A great and effective creative energy in the cosmos is the energy of visualization. If you can get yourself together to imagine and see the things that you desire from within your heart, they are likely to come true.

Sometimes you do it without even realizing that you are evoking one of the most powerful forces of the universe. If you can cultivate that, you will actually be a partner to God in creation!

How To Attract Anything You Want In Life

Every thought that passes your mind, every thing you dream of, every feeling and every desire is actually like the brick and cement with which you can construct your reality. We, as human beings, are special creatures of the Almighty and we have the power to evoke things by virtue of thought energy. The thoughts have the inherent potential to become creators of reality. Once we think our thoughts and focus on them, and nurse them with emotions, we are actually accentuating the process that will make the thought a reality. The more faith you have, the better you can carve your reality from your thoughts and desires.

There is much evidence to support this argument. You have seen how optimists have things working out the way they want it to. Haven't you ever wondered why? It is because the optimists genuinely want the best to happen. On the contrary, the pessimist has to bear with all the things that are not good, because he is always thinking about the negative. Thus, by contemplating upon the positive even pessimists can turn the tables around by concentrating on the positive.

How To Attract Anything You Want In Life

The Law Of Attraction In Business

Ever had something you really wanted fall miraculously in place? Maybe this job opportunity you desperately wanted? Or a call from the person you had been thinking of for a while? Or even a chance meeting on street with the perfect client or partner? We use various methods to describe these events. Serendipity, coincidence, Fate, karma, the advantages of being in the right place at the right time, call it what you will. All these expressions describe the result of what is generally known as the laws of attraction, commonly known as a New Age theory and the very basis of today's mantra- "Positive thinking". According to this you acquire whatever you concentrate your energy, thoughts and feelings on, positive and negative alike. A kind of self-fulfilling prophecy, it acts like a request to the universe at large and conveys what you desire most. It is like a magical mantra which will get you whatever you want, provided that you understand how this law works and utilize it to your advantage.

A very powerful mantra, the law of attraction can also affect your future adversely if you are not careful. The first step would be to be conscious of what you say.

Translating our thoughts into statements is a powerful action and directly affects our "Fate". Our statements convey not only our fears and intentions but also the vibes we exude. People often misinterpret understating their hopes/ or even self-worth to be modesty.

Sometimes it's even done to mislead the other party but by doing this; you only succeed in alienating your own good fortune. For instance- positive statements like- "I love the way my reputation attracts clients to me" or "I love the way money comes to me effortlessly in expected and unexpected ways", increases your chances of success in such cases due to the positive energy that you attract.

Failure too, is a result of such declarative statements.

The law of attraction also responds to negative declarative statements like- "I take one- step forward and two-steps back", and gives us more of them. So every time you make a negative statement, check the tendency. Simply rephrase it into something positive and promising that makes you feel better. Try this- ask yourself, "What do I want?" The moment you define what you want, you start experiencing a new mood. You seem more capable and powerful. Life will

How To Attract Anything You Want In Life

change for the better and these positive changes will become more frequent and evident. This is because you have set those universal forces in motion which determine your fate, based on your action. Recall the mood or feeling that could have lead to this. Soon you will be able to manifest more positive events and less of the unwanted ones, by using the law of attraction to your benefit.

People therefore have direct control over reality and their lives through thought alone. The trick is to be proactive.

How To Attract Anything You Want In Life

The Law Of Attraction: Does It Work?

If you are one of the people who are quite worried because the Law of Attraction doesn't work for them and have simply given up on the practice, don't lose heart.

The movie "The Secret" is an excellent representation of the law of attraction. However, many often misinterpret the movie. This misinterpretation is basically centered upon the idea that the thoughts are generating reality.

You must comprehend that it is not the thoughts themselves that make the things happen. It is the energy evolved through these thoughts that make this law work.

How effective your prayers will be is directly dependent on the amount of energy that you are able to generate by virtue of your thoughts. In fact, the amount of energy that will be generated also depends upon the amount of emotional energy that you invest in the thoughts.

Another thing that you must remember is that negative thoughts can have an adverse effect on the manifestation of your desires. This happens because the positive thoughts generate positive energy and result in the fulfillment of your desires. Since the amount of energy generated depends upon the amount of positive thoughts, negative thoughts have a negative effect and decrease the energy that is going to give shape to your desires. The negative energy cancels out the effect of the positive. Thus, when you ask for something, always do so with a frame of mind that is positive.

The more you concentrate upon your desires and think about your wish coming true, the more positive vibrations are sent to the cosmos. Try to keep that positive frame of mind consistently. In fact, if you see that negative thoughts are coming into the sphere of your thoughts then make a conscious attempt to erase them. Have faith in yourself and the universe. Try to evade doubt and you will surely get what you are yearning for.

Every day, keep some time to meditate on your desires. Select a time when you will not be disturbed by anybody and concentrate on the fulfillment of your desire. For example, if you want a great car, imagine yourself driving the car of your dreams. Put all the forces of your imagination at work and visualize your dream.

How To Attract Anything You Want In Life

Apart from the time that you spend concentrating on the desire, remember that you must not think about whether you will achieve the goal or not. As we have told you earlier, just by bringing in doubt you can undo the wonderful effects of your concentration. The negative energy has the potential to cancel out everything. So never let doubt seep into your mind. one of the best things is to begin with a desire that is not one of your immediate needs. For example, try to begin with something that will be great if you got it but is not indispensable. This is because you tend to have more doubt about the things you desperately require. If you are in great need of money, you will inevitably think about what will happen if your desires fail. This is the kind of doubt that often undoes the great work.

Thus, it is good to begin with the smaller desires. Once you are successful in achieving these little things it will give your faith a boost and improve the power of your concentration. This will enable you to focus on the bigger and more difficult things with ease later on.

Remember that the laws of desire are strange, if you can put in enough positive energy and faith, they can come true immediately. Have the faith and try to put in all the positive vibes you can gather. The results will definitely be great!

How To Attract Anything You Want In Life

The Law of Attraction And Physics

If you are one of those who think that the law of attraction is all trash, this is to remind you that these are laws of the universe that are based on the concrete foundation of scientific theory.

The Laws of Quantum physics depend upon the observation that the entire universe is composed of energy. From this, we can infer that even thoughts and abstractions are made of energy because the laws of physics have stated that the basic constituent of everything is energy. Since objects are made of energy, so are thoughts. This is the basic principle on which the Law of Attraction operates.

The Law of Attraction also professes that the energy that is contained in all abstractions are in a continuous state of vibration. The vibrations result in the production of wavelengths of various frequencies. We send these frequencies into the universe.

We send the frequencies into the vast expanse of the universe. This is, in fact, the basic principle of the Laws of Attraction.

The frequencies that we send into the universe attract the vibrations of their order. The Law of Attraction is used to attract the vibrations that are like the ones you are sending out. This law also works the other way round. If you send negative vibrations into the universe, you will attract the negative vibrations of the universe.

Laws of Attraction work on this basic principle of attracting similar vibrations.

If you concentrate on the positive vibrations, they have the power to make your dreams come true. The positive vibrations that you generate will attract other positive vibrations and result in the realization of your dreams.

Do not think that this is just dreaming for it is far more scientific and powerful than that.

You can get the lifestyle you desire for just by applying the laws of attraction. If you believe in what you desire and put in the thoughts to work, you can get all that you desire for. The Laws of Attraction have the power to make your dreams come true.

How To Attract Anything You Want In Life

In order to get the best results from your thoughts and desires, you must be really excited about them. If you constantly think about the great outcome that your desires will generate, it is bound to have some effect in the macrocosm. The better you think about it, the more effective your vibrations will become. The Laws of Attraction will result in great outcome. However, if you are somewhat unsure of your desires, you will be unable to influence the universal energy.

The Laws of Attraction will bear fruit with the correct amount of excitement generated by you. This is the key to giving shape to all the things that you dream about. Always keep in mind that negative thoughts in your part will give negative vibes to the vast universe. This is the way that the universe works and the better you understand this, the greater will be the results.

The Laws of Attraction is a wide sphere that requires a lot of study. In fact, there are many physicists who are studying the Laws of Attraction. They are studying this as a branch of science that aims at studying how the mind can exercise a lot of control on the universe.

How To Attract Anything You Want In Life

The Law Of Attraction: Think Positive

You must have heard about the Laws of Attraction. It is a new concept that has become the center of a lot of attention. There are some important facts missing in the way the Law is being publicized.

In order to understand these laws completely, you have to get a lot of information on it. there are certain things that you need to be well versed with before you can be confident about being well informed about the Laws of Attraction.

You may have heard that the key to the Laws of Attraction is positive thinking. This is somewhat true. However, there is a lot more to this theory than just positive thinking.

You must remember that your inner self is a very important part of your universe. for example, if you ask for a lot of wealth so that you will be able to help people.

Then, once the universe answers you and you end up getting a lot of wealth, you get carried away with it. you immerse yourself in all your riches and do not keep the promise that you made. This will result in the transference of your wealth to another being. This is the result in most cases.

Thus, you must remember that the external world is a manifestation of your inner self. If you concentrate on hoarding and do not develop your inner self, the universe will cease to respond to your calls. The first thing that you should do is to hone your inner being.

Remember that whatever you have will become amplified. If you are a greedy person, the greed will grow. On the other hand, if you are energetic and your soul is wealthy, the wealth will get amplified. Stop blaming the world around you. Do not try to curse your surroundings and blame the world around you. Start with changing yourself and correcting yourself.

There are certain basic laws that are in control of your world. There are certain forces that are somewhat under human control, for example, electricity. However, there are certain fixed forces like friction and gravity that are beyond human control. If you are well versed with these forces, you will be in a position of great advantage and will be able to use these laws to the best of your

How To Attract Anything You Want In Life

circumstances. However, these laws are so powerful that you can never master them completely.

The Law of Attraction is a law that helps you make your life better if you understand it to some extent. You are the master of your being and you can play a great role in the shaping up of your reality. Do not try to take the easy way and plunge into anything before fully comprehending it. Try to develop yourself and then change the way the world looks at you and the way it treats you.

If you are under the impression that using the Laws of Attraction will miraculously change your life overnight, you are quite mistaken. It definitely has the power to influence your life, but only if you know how to use it. Try to come to terms with yourself. If you are not satisfied with what you are, it will definitely take a lot of time to help yourself. You have to understand yourself, accept yourself and then try to improve your world. It might take time, but you will eventually realize that developing your inner self render your world beautiful.

The Law of Attraction In An Emergency Situation

In case you are in a dire situation and everything seems to be going wrong, do not lose heart. When everything seems to be going wrong, you have to have the courage to get over all the problems that ensnare you.

This is a time when the Laws of Attraction can help you out. You have to emit the positive vibrations that will help you get over all the problems. The positive vibrations will help you to help yourself. The thoughts and the feelings that you generate will move the universe and help you out.

Try to concentrate on your needs. Rehearse certain things. Remember what your needs are. Clearly state them in your mind. Then, try to concentrate on the feelings and imagine how you will feel if you actually attain the great things.

In the problems that are overcoming you, do not lose heart and forget that you have the power to generate the vibrations. It happens that you lose your heart to such an extent that you are unable to focus on your desires. However, do not get into the dark pits of negativity as that will only make the situation worse.

Always keep in mind that you have the power to change things. Generating the positive vibrations and shunning the negative is what a dire situation demands.

What do I want?
The general effect that bad times have on an individual is that they get into a terrible state of mind where they keep on thinking about the thing that they do not want.

Thinking about the worst things does not help at all. Get your act together and shift your concentration from all the terrible things that might happen to all the wonderful things that you want to happen. Although this is a basic step, it is a very crucial one.

What does that feel like?
After that, dream of all the great results that will have. How would you feel if all your problems were solved instantly and you got into a real great time? The more you generate such happy

How To Attract Anything You Want In Life

thoughts the better your vibrations will be.

Focus on the wonderful feeling and keep on repeating it in your mind. This will generate the vibrations that will enable you to cope with your circumstances and at the same time help you overcome them. This is how you can work out a miracle. So go ahead, and feel all that you want to make happen!

What feels good to do next?
Feeling takes you one step further to attaining the great things. The next step is to further comprehend what makes you feel better.

Ask your inner self what makes you really happy. Amidst all your trials and tribulations, try to work out a strong alternate reality that will enable you to overcome the former. Try to get the answer from your heart. It is all a matter of feelings. All the information and all the advice can not really help you. For this answer, you have to look inwards.

Get ahead of your problem and look at the solution. Do not let the many problems overpower you. Ask your inner being and you will be guided to the world where the problems are mere obstacles that cannot affect you.

Think about the great things and generate the true positive vibrations. If you are able to create this focus, there is no stopping your dreams from coming true.

How To Attract Anything You Want In Life

The Law Of Attraction Semantics

What is the use of a life that doesn't grant you happiness? Living life to the fullest is all about living a happy life, a content life, a life where you are at peace with your own personal truth. The greater the acceptance of truth on your part, the more the chance for you to experience happiness and thereby attract positive things to yourself.

Your personal belief and your personal truth are two very different concepts and you'd be best advised to not confuse one with the other. Your beliefs are ideas you have learnt from the variety of experiences you have had in your lifetime. Whereas your personal truth is something that has always existed, even before you learnt to acknowledge it.

Life is about fulfilling desires. Attracting things we desire brings us immense pleasure and pleasure is the key route to happiness. If you are yet to find happiness you probably know that it will come to you only when you manage to acquire what you desire. There is an incredible power equation between our capacity to attract and our need to be happy, as you will no doubt learn soon, neither is of value without the other.

If you have fulfilled your desire then you have probably also found your way to happiness. You have probably already realized how incredibly powerful the Law of Attraction is and how it can help you forget all your worries and achieve anything you want from life.

Before discussing further about this extraordinary potential of the Laws of Attraction let us take a brief look at a few words commonly used in this Rule of Attraction process.

Man has always been fond of inventing a number of ways of saying the same things. Thus even for a mundane enough situations as using a common salutation he has a variety of words. 'Hi', 'hello', 'Wassup', 'how are you' are various forms of the same salutation customarily used when one person meets another, and yet all of them are technically 'different' expressions. This variety is not unique to the English language alone almost all languages all over the world have a range of words meaning exactly the same thing.

Similarly, universal laws too can be expressed in a variety of ways but they will ultimately always mean the exact same thing. Take gravity for instance; all of us have our own way of

How To Attract Anything You Want In Life

defining gravity, some of us call it a 'force' others refer to it as a 'downward pull' but of course we all mean the same thing. The words we choose to express a certain idea is our own and therefore based on our personal choice regarding the structure of a sentence etc. But no matter how we express a certain idea its inherent facts always remain the same.

Semantics is an extremely important part of the Law of Attraction since it is among one of the most significant socio-spiritual laws in the universe. Like everything else people have a variety of ways of describing all spiritual experiences as well. Much like the Gravitational law the Laws of Attraction too may be described in a variety of ways, but no matter how you choose to describe it will continue to function in the same manner. We all have different names for God but ultimately the almighty is one and the same. Hence, while dealing with the Laws of Attraction and in almost every other aspect of life you'd be more likely to grasp a certain situation better only if you get past its basic semantic sense. Instead, concentrate on the inner meaning of a certain expression since that and only that will reveal to you what a certain speaker is trying to convey to you.

Communication lies at the heart of relationships so don't ignore it.

Once you brace up to this basic fact ask yourself a few relevant questions. Begin by asking yourself about the exact means by which you are attracting this particular condition or thing. Do you really want to be attracting it?

What kind of changes will this particular object/situation of desire bring about in your social, spiritual and personal life? What is keeping you from achieving this particular object/situation right at this moment? Are your personal beliefs holding you back? How serious are you about seeing this dream through to its completion level?

Are you approaching the present situation from a positive angle? How far are you willing to go to satisfy your want? What do you expect out of your desire?

What will keep you motivated enough to persevere and ultimately achieve it? Answering all these questions honestly lies at the heart of fulfilling your desires in the manner you want.

How To Attract Anything You Want In Life

The Law of Attraction: Lose Weight

We all know that like poles attract each other. Apart from being one of the most fundamental scientific laws this is also a basic law of attraction. What this law means is that people who think alike are most likely to be attracted to one another. This is based on your general get-up and your individual frame of mind. In case you think you are fat and desire to lose a bit of weight then begin by scrutinizing your inmost beliefs regarding being fat and being fit in general.

Question yourself regarding a few essential details. Do you think it is difficult to lose weight? Does your definition of fitness include depriving yourself of good food or keeping yourself hungry? Are you bogged down by your past inability to lose weight? Does exercising seem like an awful job to you? Are you intending to lose a lot of weight as quickly as possible or are you willing to be patient and make the sort of long-term changes that will keep those extra pounds away for good? Are you sure about being able to accomplish this task by means of the laws of attraction?

It's best to acknowledge that you haven't got where you stand today all at once. Events and situations have dragged you to become who you are today and what you may have become. The way you think has altered with time and experience, as has your point of view. All these have contributed to your belief system, which too has undoubtedly metamorphosed. Your extra weight is deeply related to your new set of beliefs. You can however alter these beliefs by mean of the laws of attraction and thereby change the way you presently feel about weight issues.

Everyone wants to lose weight as quickly as possible.

For the purpose a number of people use a variety of methods. Be it pills, fad diets or crash exercise programs, people are willing to go a large distance when they try to lose weight. But while all these methods might be equally effective one must remember that they are all shortcuts and that there are no shortcuts to fulfilling your desire. If you wish to lose weight and keep it off forever you ought to be ready to ditch the shortcuts and instead work hard, both at the physical as well as the mental level.

You might not be aware of it but your weight is deeply related to your mind. The laws of attraction will help you shape your mind in a way which will help you focus your entire energy on

How To Attract Anything You Want In Life

losing weight and losing weight alone. As a result you will be making the kind of decisions and engaging in the sort of activities which will help you gain a fit, well-shaped body.

Following are a few simple tricks you can use in order to let the law of attractions help you lose weight.

a. Even if you have put on a bit of weight now you know that you weren't always like this. So find a picture of yourself belonging to a time when you were slimmer. In case you can't get hold of such a picture don't lose heart, simply find a picture of someone who according to you has the sort of weight/figure you would like to attain yourself.

b. Find a few pairs of trousers that are too loose for you.

c. Tell yourself "I'm perfectly fit and in shape" continuously.

Spend sometime putting on these big clothes everyday in front of the mirror and see how slim you feel thanks to the laws of attraction. Look at how slim you look in those huge clothes and keep telling yourself "I'm perfectly fit and in shape". It's not easy to feel good about yourself and perhaps you haven't quite felt that way in a long time. But this experience ought to give you a good self-image. Do not continue with the exercise unless it does.

Remember for you to feel slim you must let go of your mental inhibitions and let yourself feel slim. Practice everyday, soon the idea will sink deep enough. It's going to take you a while to accomplish what you have set out to, so be patient. Remember, if you do stick to your routine you will soon taste success.

Do supplement your mental efforts with some concrete dietary changes as well. Eat nutritious food and count your calories, exercise often and rest enough. The results will be for everyone to see.

How To Attract Anything You Want In Life

The Law of Attraction And Parenting

You may put the Laws of Attraction to use in various facets of your life including to your duties as a parent. Everyone knows how utterly stressful parenting can be. Parenting involves a lot of responsibilities and not until you become a parent are you likely to understand exactly how many responsibilities it actually involves. For starters of course there is the responsibility of protecting your child from all possible harm. Add to that the tremendous responsibility of ensuring that your child grows up to become a respectable, responsible young adult and you'll know what we are talking about.

But parenting is not supposed to be about burdensome duties alone it also involves a lot of other far more gratifying emotions. The use of the Law of Attractions will help you realize these other aspects of parenthood as well.

Given the widespread violence in today's world it is only natural for us to be concerned about the safety of our kids. But let's face it; merely being worried will not help us save our kids from any possible harm instead it will just deteriorate our health and our mental wellness. Also remember that physical safeguarding is not all that your child needs to stay safe in today's world and that extra protection of this kind is known to do more harm than good. This is because according to the Laws of Attractions the more you think about a certain unfortunate event the more it will be likely to actually occur in your or your child's life. So if you are apprehending an accident and trying to keep your child safe from any such incident you might actually be attracting such an incident to yourself!

But relax! the Laws of Attraction will help you steer clear of such misfortune. To help your child stay safe and attain a happy life learn to think about things you want for them, rather than things you DON'T want for them. So instead of hoping that your child is not caught in a landslide or a car crash try and concentrate on thinking about how you want your child to do well in his/her class work or how you want them to win the science project. This sounds far easier than it generally turns out to be, so in case you don't succeed right at the beginning concentrate further and try harder.

How To Attract Anything You Want In Life

Begin by trying and gaining control over your emotions. Don't let your apprehensions cloud your sense of rationality. Concentrate on letting your sound judgment help you to have positive thoughts regarding your child. The greater your confidence on the fortune you want your child to be bestowed with the greater the chances of them actually coming true. Maintain your personal sense of peace at all times, the more pronounced your sense of peace the less you are likely to worry about your kids. Accept your present and face the future in a courageous manner, all these positive energies will get directed at your thoughts regarding your child and thereby keep you from being unnecessarily anxious about him/her.

Positive feelings are not easy to grasp onto especially if you are living in a particularly negative environment. In such a case you have very little choice besides changing your surrounding. If your surrounding is negative its negativity will definitely seep into your life and hold you back. This is obviously not a desirable thing.

Besides being responsible for his/her child's safety a parent is also in charge of ensuring that the child grows up to be a disciplined individual. For the purpose a parent has to often be strict about a number of things.

Punishment is important, but so is love. Even when you punish your children severely remember to forgive them and let them feel your love for them.

How To Attract Anything You Want In Life

The Law of Attraction And "The Secret"

The Laws of Attraction became particularly popular due to the famous movie called "The Secret- Law of Attraction". The movie was directed at opening people's eyes to the great potentials of thought control. A number of successful people have effectively figured out these laws all by themselves in the past. Their efficient use of these laws is what has helped them stand out in the course of history.

Every successful, wealthy person knows his/her way around the laws of attraction since they have to put these laws to use everyday in their lives. These are driven individuals who learnt early on that if they want something real bad they're most likely to get it. They are well aware that they and only they themselves have the capacity to make a change in their lives. It is this confidence upon their own selves which makes these individuals as prolific as they are.

You can put the laws of attraction to use in any aspect of your life. Whether you desire to be rich or successful or just land yourself a job, the laws of attraction can help you fulfill all your wants and more. There is no limit to the uses these laws of attraction may be put to. You can find the love of your life, get him/her to fall for you and end up achieving their eternal companionship all by means of the laws of attraction. All you need to do is wish, like they say; the universe will conspire to provide you with all that you desire provided you want it bad enough.

Consider the universe as your personal genie trapped in a bottle. Ask it for anything and watch it fulfill all your wishes provided of course you use the laws of attraction efficiently. Be careful what you wish for cause it might just come true. So select your wishes carefully and weigh the pros and the cons. Once you are sure about your desire go ahead and wish as hard as you can, there is no way you will not have it if you use the laws of attractions right.

It is amazing what the laws of attraction can do for you. And the best part is that anyone can use it. You don't need to be a saint to fulfill your wishes! all you need to be able to do is abide by the laws of attraction. If you can use the laws of attraction for your needs you will never be begging for a miracle ever again, instead you will be grasping in your hand the magic wand which will make miracles appear at every single swish. All you need to do is concentrate and really believe in your wish.

How To Attract Anything You Want In Life

There is no secret to the laws of attraction except that you must believe in it with your heart and soul. Nothing besides your personal confidence on it can make it work for you. Everyone knows about the laws of attraction but not everyone comprehends its immense potential. Also, no one understands that it's based on a principal which we refer to everyday — like poles attract each other, now everyone knows that.

How To Attract Anything You Want In Life

This Product Is Brought To You By

DAVID A OSEI

www.ingramcontent.com/pod-product-compliance
Lightning Source LLC
Chambersburg PA
CBHW020602220526
45463CB00006B/2421